I0785739

CERT Animal Response II -- Instructor Guide

978-1718793613
Original content and pictues in public domain.

CERT Animal Response II

In this module, you will learn about:

- **The Role of CERT in Responding to Animal Issues:** CERT functions that may include the handling, containment, or management of animals

- **CERT Responder Safety When Dealing With Animals:** General response when encountering animals, avoiding zoonotic disease transmission, personal protective equipment and behaviors, caring for injuries caused by animals, and psychological self-care

- **Knowledge and Skills Needed for CERT Functions That May Involve Animals:** Cleaning and disinfection, general animal care, basic animal handling, caring for injured animals, dealing with animal owners and caretakers, and animal identification and tracking

- **Sources for Additional Training and Information:** Where you can learn more about the handling and care of animals during an emergency

TABLE OF CONTENTS

PAGE

OBJECTIVES	At the conclusion of this module, the participants will be able to:

- Describe the CERT role in emergency functions that involve animals
- Describe techniques and procedures for maintaining personal safety when dealing with animals during an emergency
- Demonstrate basic skills needed to perform CERT functions that may involve animals
- Identify practices for maintaining animal safety during an emergency
- Identify sources for additional training and information

SCOPE	The topics that will be discussed in this module are:

- Module Overview
- The Role of CERT in Responding to Animal Issues
- CERT Responder Safety When Dealing With Animals
- Knowledge and Skills Needed for CERT Functions That May Involve Animals
- Sources for Additional Training and Information
- Module Summary

ESTIMATED COMPLETION TIME	4 hours

TRAINING METHODS	The lead instructor will begin by welcoming the participants to the module, introducing him- or herself and the other instructor(s), and making any necessary administrative announcements.

The instructor will begin an activity to introduce the participants to each other. Next, the instructor will briefly explain the module purpose and objectives and discuss the topics that will be covered in this session.

TRAINING METHODS (CONTINUED)

The instructor will lead a class discussion about CERT functions that may involve animals. The instructor will then introduce the topic of CERT responder safety by presenting a scenario to the class. The instructor will use images and questions to demonstrate sizeup of situations that may involve animals. Next, the instructor will present the class with information on approaching an unknown dog and use volunteers to role play the correct behavior and body language for approaching unfamiliar dogs.

Then the instructor will divide the class into two teams and lead the participants in a game on CERT safety techniques. This will allow the participants to test and share their knowledge of safety with animals. The instructor will then prompt the class to work together to generate steps for caring for injuries caused by animals. Next, the instructor will present basic knowledge and skills that CERT members will need when dealing with animals, including psychological self-care, cleaning and disinfection, general animal care, and basic animal handling techniques.

Next, the instructor will divide the class into four groups and lead a group activity that allows each group to write proper care techniques for injured-animal scenarios. The groups will share the care instructions they developed with the rest of the class, covering four different situations.

Then the instructor will present considerations when communicating with animal owners in a disaster. To help demonstrate, the instructor will use two participant volunteers to assist in a roleplay exercise that practices communication techniques for interacting with animal owners. The instructor will ask the class to critique the roleplay and then offer additional tips for communicating.

Finally, the instructor will present information on animal identification and documentation and refer participants to the sample animal documentation checklist in their Participant Manuals. The instructor will conclude the module by presenting sources for additional training and information and summarizing the topics reviewed in the module.

The instructor is encouraged to add pertinent local information to this guide but should never subtract material.

RESOURCES REQUIRED	- *CERT Animal Response II* Instructor Guide - *CERT Animal Response II* Participant Manual - *CERT Animal Response II* PowerPoint slides

EQUIPMENT

The following equipment is required for this module:

- A computer with PowerPoint software
- A computer projector and screen
- A large flip chart (easel pad) and three black markers
- Four index or laminated cards with scenarios
- Blank, lined paper
- Two bells
- Candy or animal crackers

RECOMMENDED EQUIPMENT

The following additional equipment is recommended for this module:

- A dog for demonstration of dog handling techniques
- A large stuffed dog to help demonstrate technique for approaching an unknown dog and technique for improvising a muzzle (and, depending on the construction and size, other dog restraints and carries)
- A rope to demonstrate slip leash
- A roll of 3- to 4-inch wide gauze to demonstrate improvising a muzzle

PREPARATION

Review this unit and add local information wherever requested. Prepare information on:

- Local animal facilities in your community
- Local animal wildlife in your area
- Disasters that are likely to occur locally
- Local emergency plans related to animals
- Specific animal handling techniques for animals that are prevalent in the local area
- Any system or protocol used in your community to identify dangerous animals

NOTES

A suggested time plan for this unit is as follows:

Welcome and Introductions .... 10 minutes

The Role of CERT in Responding to Animal Issues .... 20 minutes

CERT Responder Safety When Dealing With Animals .... 120 minutes

Knowledge and Skills for CERT Functions Involving Animals .... 75 minutes

Sources for Additional Training and Information .... 5 minutes

Module Summary .... 10 minutes

Total Time: 4 hours

PARTICIPANT PREREQUISITES

Participants must have completed the *CERT Basic Training* course and *CERT Animal Response I*.

INSTRUCTOR QUALIFICATIONS

Instructors for *CERT Animal Response II* should have the following qualifications:

- Completion of *CERT Basic Training* course
- Knowledge of the local Emergency Operations Plan (EOP)
- Trainer experience
- Professional experience in emergency response *and* animal handling experience — animal response, animal control, veterinary medicine, or other animal services

ACKNOWLEDGEMENTS

The national CERT Program would like to thank the following people who participated in a focus group to develop this training module:

Nancy Barr, DVM
Senior Field Veterinarian
Michigan Department of Agriculture

Robert Beckmann, Jr.
CERT Program Director
Nassau County, NY

Penny Burke
Program Specialist
Individual and Community Preparedness Division, FEMA

Anne Culver
Disaster Training Consultant
The Humane Society of the United States

Kevin Dennison, DVM
Western Regional Emergency Programs Manager
USDA APHIS Animal Care

Naomi Flam
CERT Program Instructor
Fresno, CA

Charlie O'Brien
Code Compliance Officer
Richfield (MN) Public Safety

Lt. John Reynolds
Maricopa County Animal Care and Control
Phoenix, AZ

SOURCES

- The Humane Society of the United States Disaster Animal Response Training *Personal Planning* Instructor Guide

- The Humane Society of the United States Disaster Animal Response Training *Animal Facility Planning* Instructor Guide

- The Humane Society of the United States Disaster Animal Response Training *Small Animal Behavior* Instructor Guide

- The Humane Society of the United States Disaster Animal Response Training *Exotic Animal Handling* Instructor Guide

- The Humane Society of the United States Disaster Animal Response Training *Large Animal Handling* Instructor Guide

- The Humane Society of the United States Disaster Animal Response Training *Animal First Aid* Instructor Guide

- Colorado Veterinary Medical Foundation Community Animal Response Training *Consolidated Units 1-5* Instructor Guide

- Colorado Veterinary Medical Foundation Community Animal Response Training *Unit 6 Animal Handling* Instructor Guide

- Colorado Veterinary Medical Foundation Community Animal Response Training *Unit 2 Bio-defense and Zoonoses* Instructor Guide

- Federal Emergency Management Agency (FEMA) *Information for Pet Owners* and *Information for Livestock Owners*

Notes

Notes

INSTRUCTOR GUIDANCE	CONTENT
Display Slide 0	## *Welcome and Introductions* Welcome the participants to the CERT Animal Response II supplemental training. Introduce yourselves and provide some background information about your past experiences in emergency response and animal issues. ### Introductions Develop a class roster by passing around a sheet of paper and asking participants to write down their contact information or check in on a roster created from course registration information. If there is enough time and the participants do not already know each other, ask the participants to introduce themselves by giving their names and the reason they want to learn more about animal response. ### Administrative Announcements Make any necessary administrative announcements at this time. Include information about: - Schedule of breaks for this session - Emergency exits - Restroom locations, smoking policy, etc. - Module completion requirements

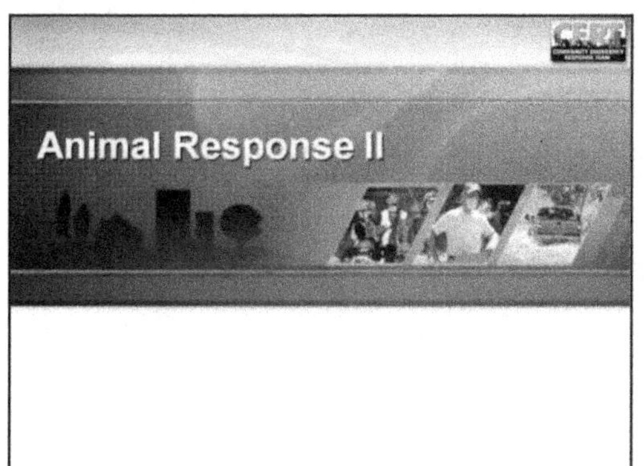

INSTRUCTOR GUIDANCE	CONTENT

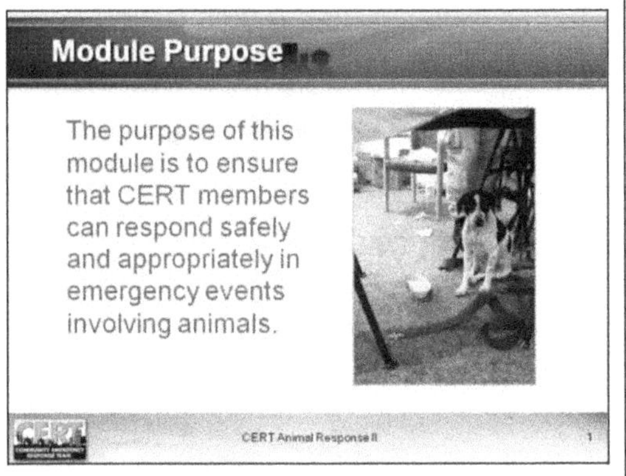

Display Slide 1

If there are CARTs, SARTs, or DARTs in your community, be prepared to provide contact information to the group.

Module Purpose

Explain that this module is the second of two modules that make up the CERT Animal Response training. Read the purpose of this module, *Animal Response II*:

The purpose of this module is to ensure that CERT members can respond safely and appropriately in emergency events involving animals.

Explain that the CERT supplemental training on animals is meant to support the disaster response training they've already received in the *CERT Basic Training* course. In terms of disaster response, the focus of this module will be preparation for situations involving animals that they may encounter in performing their broader CERT response functions.

Note that this is different from training for volunteer response teams such as County or Community Animal Response Teams (CARTs), State Animal/Agricultural Response/Resource Teams (SARTs), or Disaster Animal Response Teams (DARTs). The mission of these types of teams is specifically State and local preparedness, resource management, and animal response during disasters.

Also, caution participants that this training will not make them competent professional animal handlers.

Course Materials

Explain that the Participant Manual outlines the material to be covered, including the presentations, group activities, and exercises. Note that the Participant Manual is intended to complement, but cannot substitute for attending the classroom delivery of the module. Each person will keep their copy of the Participant Manual and should feel free to make notes in their copy.

INSTRUCTOR GUIDANCE	CONTENT

Display Slide 2

Animal Categories

Remind participants that the material in this module, like the material in *Animal Response I*, is intended to generally cover six categories of animals:

- Household pets, domesticated animals such as a dog, cat, bird, rabbit, rodent, or turtle that is kept in the home for pleasure rather than commercial purposes

- Service animals, trained to assist people with disabilities, etc.

- For-profit animals, including livestock and commercial animals such as those bred and/or trained for sale or other profit

- Non-commercial livestock such as horses kept for personal recreation

- Wildlife, those wild animals indigenous to an area

- Exotic animals, which may be pets

Considerations specific to a particular category of animals are identified in the material.

Display Slide 3

What You Will Learn

List the topics that will be learned in the module:

- The Role of CERT in Responding to Animal Issues

- CERT Responder Safety When Dealing With Animals

- Knowledge and Skills Needed for CERT Functions That May Involve Animals

- Sources for Additional Training and Information

INSTRUCTOR GUIDANCE	CONTENT
 **Display Slide 4**   **Display Slide 5**	**Module Objectives** At the end of this module, participants should be able to: • Describe the CERT role in emergency functions that involve animals • Describe techniques and procedures for maintaining personal safety when dealing with animals during an emergency • Demonstrate basic skills needed to perform CERT functions that may involve animals • Identify practices for maintaining animal safety during an emergency • Identify sources for additional training and information

INSTRUCTOR GUIDANCE	CONTENT

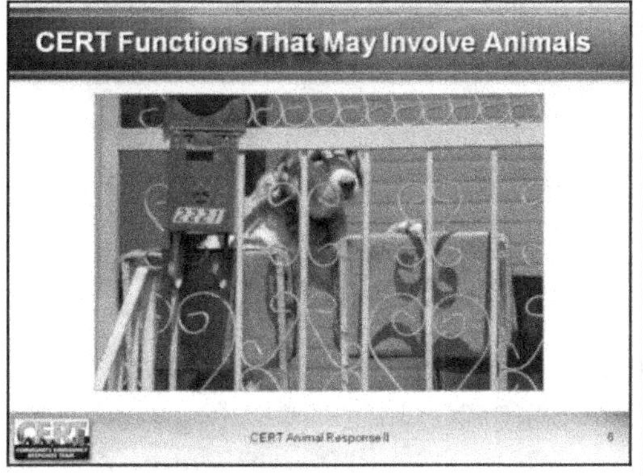

Display Slide 6

The Role of CERT in Responding to Animal Issues

Introduce the next topic, "The Role of CERT in Responding to Animal Issues."

As a CERT member, what emergency functions do you perform that could involve animals?

Record responses on easel pad or whiteboard. Suggested responses:

- Assessing damage

- Managing interrupted utilities

- Setting up and operating Team's command post

- Assisting animal rescue

- Evacuating people who own animals

- Searching buildings

- Working emergency hotlines

- Rescuing and treating injured people

- Assisting in an emergency animal shelter

- Supporting local animal response or response personnel

- Coordinating between animal and human shelters

The Role of CERT in Responding to Animal Issues

INSTRUCTOR GUIDANCE	CONTENT

	Lead a group discussion by covering any of the following information not already mentioned by the class.
	
	CERT Functions That May Involve Animals
	- Animal-related tasks that may arise when conducting primary CERT tasks
	  - Responding to unaccompanied or displaced animals encountered during damage assessment, search and rescue assignments, or dealing with interrupted utilities
	  - Setting up or operating the team command post
	- Assisting in setting up and operating local existing and emergency animal shelters
	  - Record management
	- Augmenting and supporting the local animal response program
	  - Community Animal Response Team (CART)
	  - State Animal Response Team (SART)
	  - Disaster Animal Response Team (DART)
	- Helping to evacuate neighbors and community members who own animals
	- Communicating animal information for emergency hotlines
	- Animal transport
	- Coordination between emergency animal shelters and human shelters

INSTRUCTOR GUIDANCE	CONTENT

Display Slide 7

CERT Responder Safety When Dealing with Animals

Introduce the next topic, "CERT Responder Safety When Dealing With Animals."

Explain that in the variety of situations where CERT members may encounter animals, rescuer safety is the number one priority.

Explain that this topic on responder safety will cover:

- Encountering Animals
- Zoonotic Disease Transmission
- Injuries Caused by Animals
- Psychological Self-Care

Display Slide 8

Suggested response:

- Size up the situation

Read this scenario:

Your community was evacuated due to a wildfire that passed through the area. Your CERT is supporting disaster responders in assessing damage to the community. You have been asked to assist animal control in searching the damaged home of a woman who is rumored to breed pit bull terriers.

As a trained CERT member, what is the first thing you will do as you near the house?

INSTRUCTOR GUIDANCE	CONTENT
	Encountering Animals **How can you size up a situation that may involve animals?**
Suggested responses: - Look for presence of owner. - Look for evidence of animals. - Consider local environment. - Be prepared for illegal animal activity. - Perform damage assessment.	

Display Slide 9

Stress the importance of always sizing up the situation before entering an unknown area or home. Emphasize that sizing up the situation is imperative whenever animals could be in the area.

Review the steps for sizing up a situation that may involve animals:

1. Look for the presence of the owner.
2. Look for evidence of animals.
3. Consider the local environment.
4. Be prepared for potential illegal animal activity.
5. Perform damage assessment.

CERT Responder Safety when Dealing with Animals

INSTRUCTOR GUIDANCE	CONTENT
 Display Slide 10 Call on a few volunteers to answer. Suggested responses: - Car in front of the house - Open window Suggested responses: - Ring the doorbell or knock on the door. - Search the sides and back of the house. - If the door is unlocked or windows are open, yell, "Is anyone home?" - Ask neighbors.	<u>1. Look for Presence of the Owner.</u> Stress that it is best for the owner to handle or provide instruction regarding his or her own animals rather than for you and your team members to guess at what you might find or handle unknown animals on your own. Read this scenario: A heavy storm damaged many homes in your community. You are assisting local emergency responders in assessing damage to the homes in one district of the community. **Do you see evidence in this picture that an owner may be on the property?** **What else can you do to determine if an owner is present?**

CERT Responder Safety when Dealing with Animals

INSTRUCTOR GUIDANCE	CONTENT
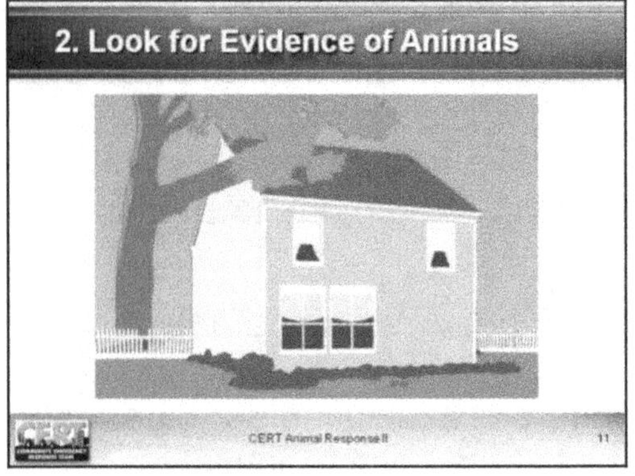**Display Slide 11** Call on volunteers to answer. Suggested responses: - Animal cages - Fences - Stables or pens - Animal food bowls or troughs - Animal toys - Sounds of animals - Other signs such as feathers or fur balls	2. Look for Evidence of Animals. **Do you see any clues in this picture that indicate the presence of animals?**
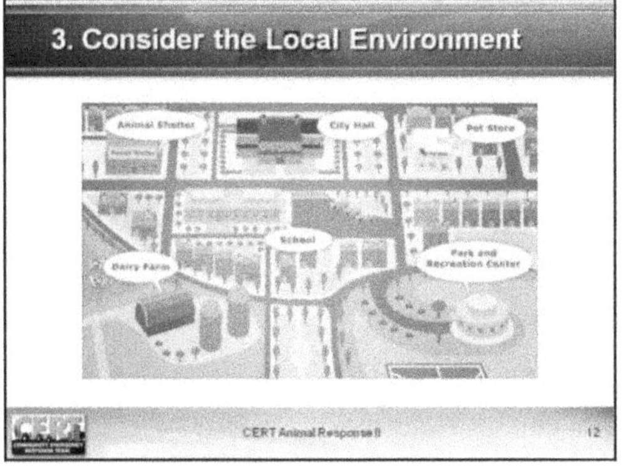**Display Slide 12**	3. Consider the Local Environment.

CERT Responder Safety when Dealing with Animals

INSTRUCTOR GUIDANCE	CONTENT
	What types of facilities might house animals?
Suggested responses: ■ Farms ■ Agricultural industries ■ Racetracks ■ Zoos ■ Wildlife rehab centers ■ Animal shelters ■ Kennels ■ Pet stores ■ Animal research laboratories	
	What animal facilities are located in your area?
Suggested responses: Insert local animal facilities in your community.	
	What types of animals might be encountered?
Suggested responses: Insert animals that may be encountered in your community.	
Add list of animals common in the local natural environment.	Ask participants to consider local wildlife as well. Name some animals that are common in the natural environment surrounding your community. Remind participants that these animals could become displaced during or after a disaster.

INSTRUCTOR GUIDANCE	CONTENT

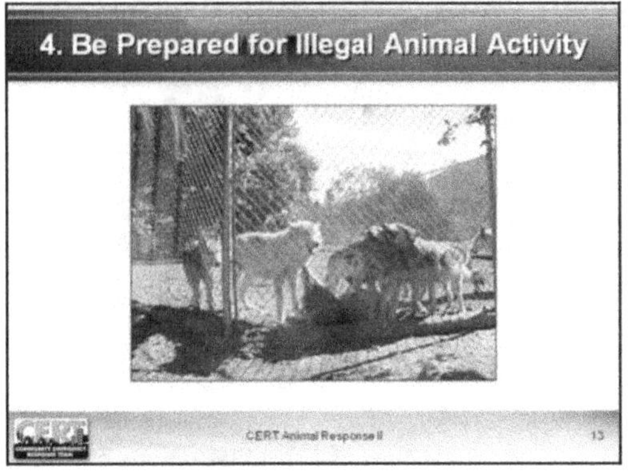
Display Slide 13
 	
Call on a few volunteers to answer. Suggested responses:
 	
▪ Animal hoarding
 	
▪ Animal fighting
 	
▪ Illegal exotic animal breeding
	<u>4. Be Prepared for Illegal Animal Activity.</u>
	
	What are some types of illegal animal activity you could encounter during a disaster response?
	
	Cover the following information:
	
	▪ Animal hoarding
	
	   • The owner may be housing a large number of pets that he or she is unable to care for.
	
	   • They are usually dogs and cats but could be more exotic animals such as snakes, rabbits, large cats, or alligators.
	
	   • Hundreds of animals may be kept in extremely unsanitary conditions. (The property may be covered in animal feces and decomposing carcasses.)
	
	   • Animals may be severely neglected, malnourished, or sick.
	
	▪ Animal fighting
	
	   • Animals are bred and trained to fight each other, often to their death.

CERT Responder Safety when Dealing with Animals

INSTRUCTOR GUIDANCE	CONTENT
	<ul><li>Animals may be dangerous to handle.</li><li>Illegal fighting animals that may be encountered include:<ul><li>Roosters</li><li>Dogs (usually pit bulls)</li><li>Hogs for hog-dog fighting</li></ul></li></ul><ul><li>Illegal exotic animal breeding or possession of illegal exotic wildlife (non-native) and illegally kept native wildlife<ul><li>State and local laws concerning exotic animal and captive native wildlife species vary widely. Local animal control and State wildlife agencies can help identify illegal species.</li><li>These animals are not domesticated; they are still wild animals, and some species may be very dangerous.</li><li>They may carry zoonotic disease (all species).</li><li>Examples of exotic wildlife privately owned (legal and illegal) include:<ul><li>5,000 privately owned tigers in the U.S.</li><li>Monkeys and apes</li><li>Reptiles and amphibians such as iguanas, other lizards, snakes (small, large, very large, and poisonous), turtles, and frogs</li><li>Hedgehogs, sugar gliders, and small non-threatening species</li></ul></li><li>Examples of native wildlife species that may be kept as pets or bred include:<ul><li>Wolves and wolf hybrids</li><li>Foxes</li><li>Skunks (illegal in most States)</li><li>Raccoons</li><li>Raptors</li><li>Reptiles and amphibians (alligators, snakes, lizards, frogs, salamanders)</li></ul></li></ul></li></ul>

CERT Responder Safety when Dealing with Animals

INSTRUCTOR GUIDANCE	CONTENT
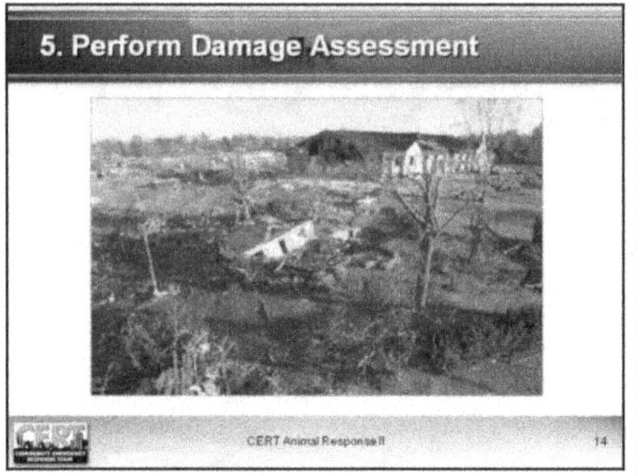 **Display Slide 14** Suggested responses: - Survey damage to animal facilities. - Contact local animal facilities and emergency management. - Find out whether there are individual animals in need. - Determine the impact on animal owners. - Verify initial reports on animal impact.	5. Perform Damage Assessment. **How might the damage assessment process be different if the situation involves animals?** Explain that overall assessment of damage that could involve animals will be the responsibility of many different responders, including emergency response agencies, animal control agencies, animal advocacy organizations, emergency managers, and CERT. Explain that, having sized up the situation, CERT members will be more prepared for encounters with animals. Remind them again that, as always, responder safety is the top priority. Tell the group that because responders may frequently encounter dogs, the next section will cover safety precautions around unknown dogs.

INSTRUCTOR GUIDANCE	CONTENT

Approaching an Unknown Dog
 	
• Expect the unexpected
• Do not let dog block your escape
• Do not show fear
• Maintain relaxed posture
• Control environment if possible
• Avoid direct eye contact
• Do not get near dog's face
 	
CERT Animal Response II   15
 	
Display Slide 15
	Approaching an Unknown Dog
	
	Present this information:
	
	Although dogs are domesticated animals, they are natural predators and may revert to instinctive behavior, such as chasing or attacking, if frightened or provoked.
	
	An animal that is faced with an emergency situation or that has survived a disaster may display uncharacteristic behavior for a time.
	
	When approaching an unknown dog, keep in mind that some dogs may be trained as watchdogs or attack dogs. Always consider the safety of yourself, your team members, and others in the area before attempting to handle or manage an unknown animal.
	
	When approaching any dog, remember these points:
	
	▪ Always expect the unexpected.
	
	▪ Do not allow the dog between you and your escape route.
	
	▪ Do not show fear.
	
	▪ Maintain a relaxed posture.
	
	   • Present the side rather than the front of your body.
	
	   • Avoid standing or looming over the dog.
	
	   • Use a soft voice.
	
	▪ Control the environment if possible.
	
	   • Avoid loud noises.
	
	   • Turn off flashing lights.
	
	   • Minimize the number of people in the area.
	
	▪ Avoid direct eye contact.
	
	▪ Do not get near the dog's face.

CERT Responder Safety when Dealing with Animals

INSTRUCTOR GUIDANCE	CONTENT

	<u>Exercise: Approaching a Dog Roleplay</u>
	
	<u>Purpose:</u> The purpose of this exercise is to demonstrate the proper way to approach an unknown dog.
	
	<u>Instructions:</u> Follow the steps below to conduct the exercise:
	
	1. Ask a volunteer to demonstrate appropriate body language for approaching a dog by maintaining a relaxed posture and avoiding eye contact.
	
	2. You can pretend that you are the dog and let the volunteer approach you.
	
	3. As the dog, maintain a stance that shows you are standing your ground, but do not act aggressively.
	
	4. If the volunteer behaves in the correct manner, you can relax your stance a little as the volunteer approaches or begin to sniff the volunteer's hand.
	
	5. If the volunteer behaves incorrectly, as in looming over you, speaking loudly, or nearing your face, become aggressive and bark loudly or snap at the volunteer as if you are trying to bite.
	
	6. Ask the rest of the class to critique the volunteer's behavior, and add your own comments or corrections when needed.
	
	7. Comment on whether the volunteer maintained each of these behaviors:
	
	  • Showed relaxed posture
	
	  • Presented side of body
	
	  • Did not stand over the dog
	
	  • Used a soft voice
	
	  • Avoided direct eye contact
	
	  • Avoided getting near the dog's face

INSTRUCTOR GUIDANCE	CONTENT
	Debrief: Debrief by emphasizing the importance of approaching an unknown animal carefully and according to your training in order to avoid a dangerous situation.
Approaching an Unknown Dog (cont'd) • Try gaining dog's confidence • Try to contain dog • Consider size of your team • Know your limitations CERT Animal Response II **Display Slide 16**	Tell the class that another way to maintain control of a situation is to gain the animal's confidence. You can do this by offering a treat or a toy or attempting basic one-word obedience commands.

Explain the following about offering treats or toys:

- If dog treats are available, gently toss a treat to the ground near the dog. Minimize arm and hand movement when you toss the treat. Do not offer a treat by hand.

- Do not attempt to pick up one of the dog's toys; however, if you have a tennis ball, consider engaging the dog with it.

  - First check to see if there is a safe area into which you could toss the tennis ball. The area should be on either side of you (not behind you) and safe for the dog. Be certain that the tennis ball will not lead the dog toward the street even if there doesn't appear to be any traffic.

  - Bounce the tennis ball a couple of times. If the dog seems interested, toss the tennis ball into the safe area and wait for the dog to chase it.

Tell the group that, in some cases, another way to gain the animal's confidence is by using one-word obedience commands. |

INSTRUCTOR GUIDANCE	CONTENT
	Does anyone know the basic command for "Sit"?
Suggested volunteer demonstration:	Ask a volunteer to demonstrate the proper technique for the class. Comment on the demonstration as it occurs. The technique should include:
▪ Say "Sit" firmly but not loudly	▪ Saying "Sit" firmly but not loudly, and
▪ Hold your hand in a "Stop" gesture	▪ Holding one's hand in a "Stop" gesture
• Arm straight out	• Arm straight out
• Hand perpendicular to the floor	• Hand perpendicular to the floor
• Palm facing out	• Palm facing out
	If the volunteer does the command incorrectly, add corrections and demonstrate the proper technique yourself.

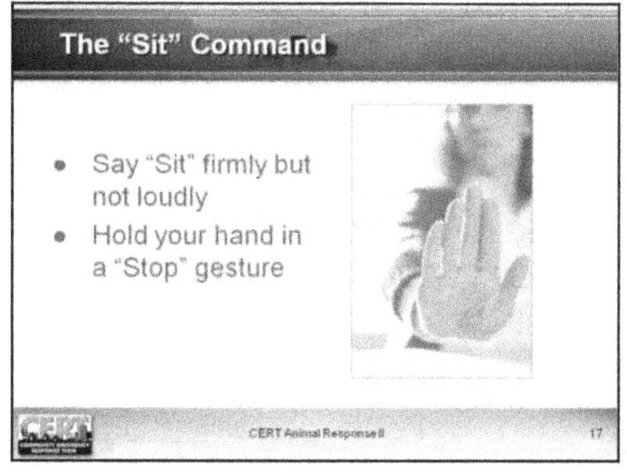

Display Slide 17

Add that you can also control the situation by containing or confining the dog in a separate part of the yard. Do this only if you feel comfortable and the animal is not behaving aggressively.

Without making physical contact, place a slip leash over the dog's head. Do not attempt to attach a leash to a collar as you could end up holding an empty leash and collar and chasing the dog.

Note that the use of slip leashes will be covered in more detail later in the module.

<u>Important Notes</u>

▪ If at any time you do not feel comfortable handling the dog, call animal control or a team member who is more experienced with animals.

▪ Before trying to manage an unknown dog, consider the size of your team. It is best to have at least three people.

▪ Know your limitations. Some animals may be better off left alone.

CERT Responder Safety when Dealing with Animals

INSTRUCTOR GUIDANCE	CONTENT
If a Dog Attacks • In the event of any dog attack, call 911 immediately • Use basic commands • Put object or distance between yourself and dog • Back away; do not run away • If you fall, curl up and cover your head • Do not scream or yell • If dog latches on, protect your face CERT Animal Response II 18 **Display Slide 18**	<u>If a Dog Attacks</u> If you are ever attacked or about to be attacked by a dog or if you witness the attack of another person, follow these rules: ▪ Call for help immediately. If you witness an attack on another person, first call 911 for help. If you are attacked, call 911 for help as soon as possible. ▪ You may be able to stop a dog that is in attack mode by using basic commands. ▪ Put an object or distance between the dog and yourself. You can use a backpack, notebook, or any other object on hand. ▪ If available, use pepper spray on the dog. ▪ Back away; never run away. ▪ If you fall down, curl up in a ball and cover your head. ▪ Do not scream or yell. ▪ If the dog latches on, protect your face and neck. **Zoonotic Disease Transmission and Personal Protective Equipment and Behaviors** Tell participants that now that they have learned how to approach and handle dogs, we will discuss how to use personal protective equipment (PPE) and other protective behavior to avoid the spread of zoonotic disease when dealing with animals. Caution participants by telling them that as CERT members, they must exercise all precautions when handling animals. This includes using protective behavior and equipment to avoid the spread of zoonotic disease to themselves and their families. Tell participants to remember that any unknown animal may carry an infectious disease, even with no visible symptoms. Then explain that you will now conduct a game that

CERT Responder Safety when Dealing with Animals

INSTRUCTOR GUIDANCE	CONTENT

	will introduce participants to the concepts of zoonotic disease. Let participants know that you have not yet covered this information, but you would like to see how much everyone knows about personal protective behavior and how they apply it to functions involving animals. Explain that participants will learn about the topic throughout the game.
	
	CERT Safety Game
	
	Purpose: This exercise allows participants to learn about zoonotic disease transmission and protective behaviors and to share information with each other.
	
	Instructions: Follow the steps below to conduct the exercise.
	
	1. Divide the class into two teams and give each team a bell.
	
	2. Ask participants to close their Participant Manuals for the game and let them open them after the game to review the answers.
	
	3. Explain the rules of the game:
	
	  • After you ask each question, you will call on whichever team rings the bell first.
	
	  • The participant who rings the bell gets to answer the question. If the participant answers correctly, his or her team receives 100 points.
	
	  • If the participant answers incorrectly, another participant from the same team can try to answer the same question. If the second participant answers correctly, you will give his or her team 100 points.
	
	  • If he or she answers incorrectly, you will subtract 50 points from the team's score and provide the correct answer or answers. (Make sure you discuss all of the answers listed on

INSTRUCTOR GUIDANCE	CONTENT
	the next page.)
	4. Make sure the game is fast paced, but use detailed feedback to help participants learn the material. Depending on the types of answers you receive, you may need to clarify a participant's response with your own explanation. Explain why an answer is correct or incorrect while keeping your explanation no longer than two or three sentences to avoid slowing the pace of the game.
	5. Ask each question listed below. Keep track of each team's score on your easel pad or whiteboard.
	6. Pass out a bag of candy or candy bars (or animal crackers) to the winning team.
	7. Be sure to tell participants to re-open their Participant Manuals before you begin your final summary of the material covered in the game. This will give them a chance to record the correct answers.
Answers to game questions:	Game Questions:
1. An infectious disease that spreads naturally between animals and people	1. What is zoonotic disease?
2. Any three of the following: orally, direct contact with animal, inhalation (airborne), through a vector (living organism), through an intermediary object (fomite)	2. Name three ways zoonotic disease can be transmitted.
3. Leash, collar, food or water bowl, animal brush	3. Name an inanimate object that could carry a zoonotic disease.

INSTRUCTOR GUIDANCE	CONTENT
4. Tick, mosquito	4. Name the two organisms that are most likely to spread zoonotic disease.
5. Washing hands (with soap and water or hand sanitizer)	5. What is the most important hygienic behavior you can use to prevent the spread of zoonotic disease?
6. Use insect repellent; reduce standing water where possible.	6. What can you do to prevent the spread of vector-borne disease?
7. Avoid hand-to-mouth contact when around animals; change clothes and footwear before going home; shower if possible before going home.	7. What is another hygienic behavior that will prevent the spread of zoonotic disease?
8. Your CERT supervisor and a medical officer or doctor	8. If you are bitten or injured by an animal during CERT operations, to whom should you report the bite?
9. Let your physician know that you had contact with an animal.	9. If you become ill after contact with an animal, what should you do?
10. Any three of the following: helmet, goggles or eye protection, N-95 mask, heavy leather work gloves, nitrile gloves, appropriate clothing and footwear	10. List three pieces of standard CERT personal protective equipment (PPE).
11. No, because your foot could be severely injured by the steel if a heavy animal steps on your toes	11. Yes or no: Is it a good idea to wear steel-toed boots when handling large animals?

CERT Responder Safety when Dealing with Animals

INSTRUCTOR GUIDANCE	CONTENT
12. Hand sanitizer or insect repellent	12. Aside from standard CERT PPE, what is another PPE item you should carry with you if you expect to be handling or encountering animals?
13. Any of the following: slip leashes for dogs, treats, tennis ball, pillowcase for transporting cats	13. Name an item you should carry with you if you expect to have contact with animals.

Ask if anyone has any questions or comments about zoonotic disease or personal protective equipment.

Tell the class to open their Participant Manuals to the game questions (p. 14-15). Summarize the material learned in the game and facilitate further discussion on any points that participants had trouble with or that need further clarification. Conclude the game by telling participants they should use information shared during this game to protect their safety during an emergency response.

Treatment for Injuries Caused by Animals

Read this scenario:

You and two other CERT members have spent the entire day evacuating animals from a pet shop that was partially destroyed by an earthquake. You have run out of cat carriers and need to use a pillowcase to transport a Persian kitten. The kitten bites your wrist as you attempt to place it inside the pillowcase. The bite is small but draws blood. You don't want to stop and care for the bite because there are only a few animals left that need to be evacuated.

What should you do?

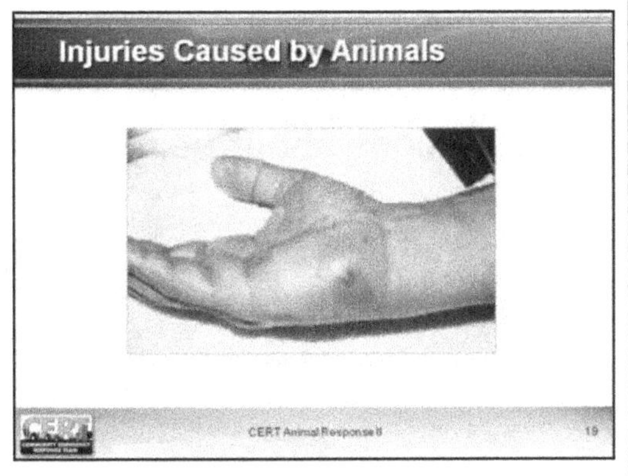

Display Slide 19

Suggested responses:

CERT Responder Safety when Dealing with Animals

INSTRUCTOR GUIDANCE	CONTENT
1. Wash any animal scratch, bite, or injury immediately with soap and water. 2. Administer first aid as appropriate. 3. Seek immediate attention for any bite. 4. If rabies is possible, have the animal captured for testing or quarantine. Report all injuries to your CERT supervisor immediately.	Discuss the responses and any other appropriate actions that may not have been mentioned. Caution participants that rabies in humans is always fatal if left untreated. The World Health Organization estimates that approximately 55,000 people die from rabies each year throughout the world. Fatality by rabies occurs when people do not receive vaccination after being bitten by a rabid animal. *"Fact Sheet No. 99." World Health Organization. December, 2008.* **Ask if there are any questions about treating animal-caused injuries.**

CERT Responder Safety when Dealing with Animals

INSTRUCTOR GUIDANCE	CONTENT

Psychological Self-Care

- Working with animals can be emotional
- Responders may be affected by emotions of animal owners
- Do not push yourself beyond your limits
- Animals can also reduce stress
- See *CERT Basic Training* Unit 7 Disaster Psychology

CERT Animal Response II   20

Display Slide 20

Psychological Self-Care

Emphasize that CERT members should be aware of the psychological impact of dealing with animals.

- Working with animals can be particularly emotional because animals are helpless in the face of disaster.

- Responders may be affected by the stress of animal owners who have lost their pets or their livestock and livelihood.

- Be careful not to push yourself beyond your limits because there are too many animals in need; you still need to rest, eat, and sleep.

- Note that positive interaction with animals can also reduce stress.

Encourage participants to refer back to *CERT Basic Training* Unit 7 on Disaster Psychology.

Knowledge and Skills Needed for CERT Functions That May Involve Animals

- This topic will cover:
  - Cleaning and Disinfection
  - General Animal Care
  - Animal Handling
  - Caring for Injured Animals
  - Communicating with Animal Owners
  - Animal Identification and Documentation

CERT Animal Response II   21

Display Slide 21

Knowledge and Skills Needed for CERT Functions That May Involve Animals

Introduce the next topic, "Knowledge and Skills Needed for CERT Functions Involving Animals." Refer participants to p. 17 of the Participant Manual.

Explain that participants should now understand their role in emergency functions involving animals and how to protect themselves if they encounter animals during a CERT activation. This topic will set them up with the basic skills they need to perform CERT functions involving animals, animal owners, and animal equipment.

INSTRUCTOR GUIDANCE	CONTENT
	Explain that this topic will cover: - Cleaning and Disinfection - General Animal Care - Animal Handling - Caring for Injured Animals - Communicating with Animal Owners - Animal Identification and Documentation **Cleaning and Disinfection** **What animal-related housing or equipment do you think you may need to clean as part of your CERT duties?**
Suggested responses: - Cages - Food and water bowls - Boots and clothing - Hazardous area - Animal transport vehicles	

Display Slide 22	Cover the following cleaning and disinfection procedure:
	1. Debris and organic material MUST be removed as soon as possible from cages, food and water bowls, footwear, and clothing.
	2. Clean with soap and water (disinfectant will not work in the presence of organic material).
	3. Apply a suitable disinfectant (follow label directions).
	  - You can make disinfectant by diluting household bleach with water:
	    30 parts water to 1 part bleach
	  - To disinfect properly, you must maintain 10 minutes of contact time before rinsing.

CERT Knowledge and Skills Involving Animals

INSTRUCTOR GUIDANCE	CONTENT

General Animal Care
• Follow nutritional and environmental requirements
• Not feeding animal is better than feeding wrong food
• All animals need clean and potable water
• Store feed where animals can't access
 	
Display Slide 23
	General Animal Care
	
	Cover the following information:
	
	■ Each species has its own nutritional and environmental requirements; these should be kept in mind even during a disaster.
	
	■ It's better not to feed the animal anything than to feed it the wrong food.
	
	■ All animals need clean and potable water.
	
	   • For large quantities of water:
	
	      • Cloudy water: 15 gallons of water to 1 tablespoon of unperfumed household bleach
	
	      • Clear water: 15 gallons of water to 1½ teaspoons of unperfumed household bleach
	
	   • For smaller quantities of water:
	
	      • Cloudy water: 1 gallon of water to ¼ teaspoon of unperfumed household bleach
	
	      • Clear water: 1 gallon of water to 1/8 teaspoon of unperfumed household bleach
	
	   • A higher concentration of bleach can be toxic.
	
	■ Store all feed securely where animals cannot get to it.
	
	■ Hoofed livestock may be especially vulnerable to life-threatening complications from improper feeding.
	
	■ After assistance is provided during an emergency, pets and livestock need to be returned to their owners to establish a return to normalcy.

INSTRUCTOR GUIDANCE	CONTENT
	Animal Handling: Dogs Stress that it is essential for participants to get to know the body language of animals they handle. Refer participants to the *CERT Animal Response I* module for information on animal behavior and body language. **If a dog is not showing aggression, how can you handle it?**
Suggested responses: • Avoid prolonged direct eye contact. • Use soft voice. • Approach dog with your body turned sideways. • Move toward the dog slowly. • To control the dog, use a slip leash. • Do not loom over dog. • Do not grab dog by collar.	
Display Slide 24	Review the information on the slide that was not already covered by the class.

CERT Knowledge and Skills Involving Animals

CERT Knowledge and Skills Involving Animals

INSTRUCTOR GUIDANCE	CONTENT

Display Slide 25

Review the following information.

<u>Handling frightened dogs</u>

- Seek assistance unless you are an experienced dog handler.

- Don't approach dogs unless there are people nearby who can assist you.

- Move slowly and, if possible, get the dog to come to you.

<u>Handling aggressive dogs</u>

- Call animal control or law enforcement.

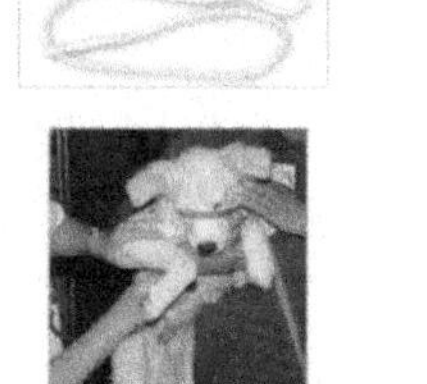

Display Slide 26

If possible, the techniques for handling a dog should be demonstrated in the classroom with a live dog. A live demonstration would be especially useful in training participants on the various dog restraints and how to carry a dog. Use a large stuffed dog if a live dog is not available.

<u>Dog Restraints: Leashes</u>

- Use a leash only if the dog is not behaving aggressively.

- If given time, some aggressive dogs may calm down and can then be handled on leash.

- Keep the dog calm before and during the time you slip the leash over its head.

- Slip leashes that loop around the dog's neck and slip to tighten are the most secure and effective.

- You can improvise a leash by using rope, twine, wire, or a belt.

CERT Knowledge and Skills Involving Animals

INSTRUCTOR GUIDANCE	CONTENT

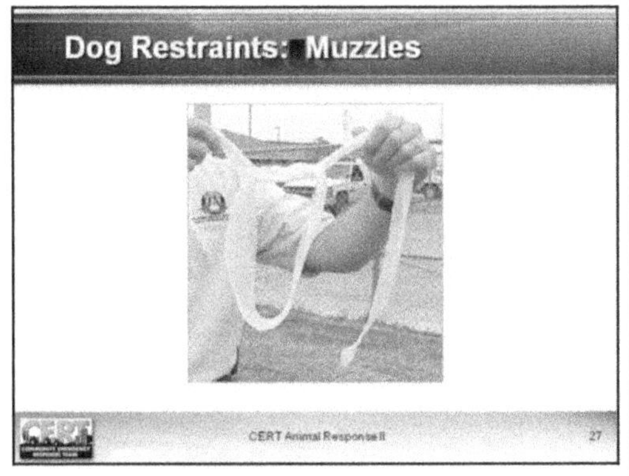
 	
Display Slide 27
	Dog Restraints: Muzzles
	
	• Used to prevent dogs from biting
	• To improvise a temporary muzzle:
	
	    • Begin with a roll of 3- to 4-inch-wide gauze (doubled for strength) or a piece of rope 3 to 4 feet long.
	
	    • Have someone else restrain the dog's head as you slip a loop in the middle of the material around the dog's nose.
	
	    • Tighten the loop around the dog's closed mouth.
	
	    • Loop the rope downward on each side and tie it under the dog's nose and mouth.
	
	    • Maintain tension and tie the ends of the rope around the back of the dog's head, securing with a simple tie knot and bow.
	
	    • Muzzles should be tied securely but for easy release; the dog should be able to breathe through its nose.
	
	    • Until the dog is otherwise contained or controlled (caged, leashed), you must continue to restrain the dog's head and front legs or it will immediately remove the muzzle.
	
	    • Note: This muzzle will not work on cats and short-nosed dogs such as pugs.

CERT Knowledge and Skills Involving Animals

INSTRUCTOR GUIDANCE	CONTENT

Dog Restraints: Standing

1. Place arm under dog's neck and other arm behind rear legs
2. Pull dog's head snugly against your shoulder

CERT Animal Response II

Display Slide 28

Dog Restraints: Standing

Explain that in some cases, for example when administering first aid to an injured animal, they may need to restrain the animal. This can be done either in a standing or a prone position. Demonstrate the steps below for restraining a dog in a standing position, describing each step as you demonstrate. Use a real dog if you have one available for the class.

To restrain a standing dog, either on the ground or on a table:

1. Place one arm under the dog's neck and your other arm behind the rear legs or under the dog's abdomen.

2. Pull the dog's head snugly against your shoulder.

Dog Restraints: Lateral

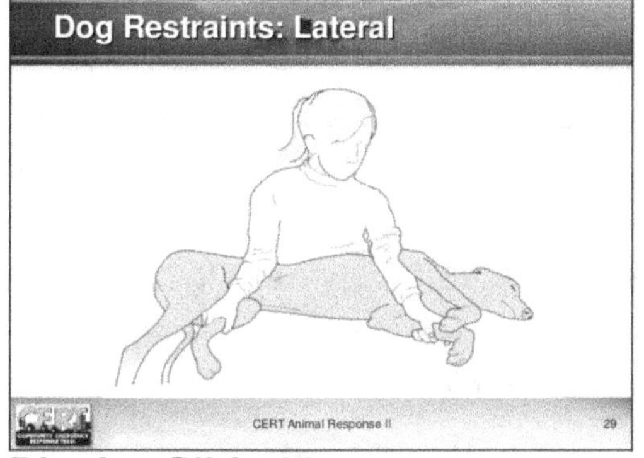

CERT Animal Response II

Display Slide 29

Dog Restraints: Lateral

Demonstrate the steps below for restraining a dog in a lateral position, either on the ground or on a table, describing each step as you demonstrate. Use a real dog if you have one available for the class.

To restrain a dog in a lateral position:

1. Place one arm around the front of the dog, holding the leg on the opposite side of you.

2. Place your other arm around the dog's hind-quarters, also holding the opposite leg.

3. Pull the dog snugly against your body.

4. Lift the dog up and, holding it snugly, bend over to gently lay the dog on its side.

5. Maintain a hold on the dog while moving to the back of the dog.

6. Hold the dog's bottom legs down against the ground, placing your elbows across the dog's hips and neck, as shown on the slide.

CERT Knowledge and Skills Involving Animals

INSTRUCTOR GUIDANCE	CONTENT
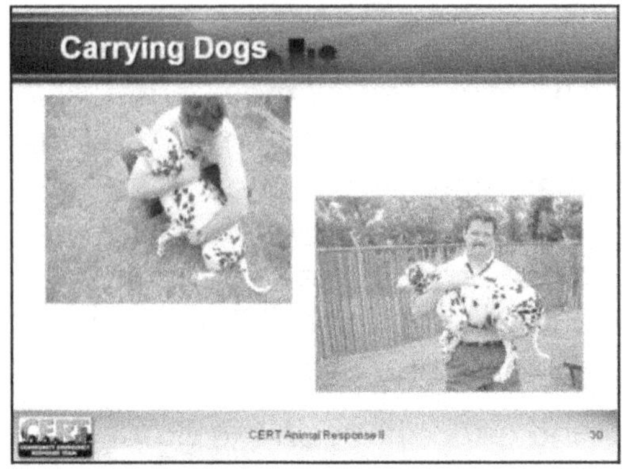 **Display Slide 30**	**Carrying Dogs** Demonstrate the steps below for carrying a dog, describing each step as you demonstrate. Use a real dog if you have one available for the class. ▪ Support the chest and hindquarters as you lift the dog. ▪ Note: If the dog's back or hindquarters have been injured, this type of lifting could be painful, but you should still proceed. ▪ If a dog shows any indication of fear or aggression, it should be muzzled prior to lifting.
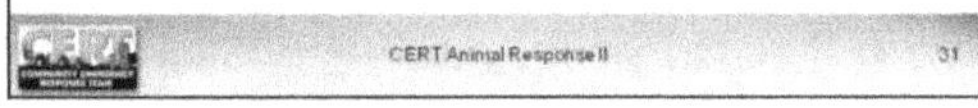 **Display Slide 31**	**Transporting Dogs** Cover the following information: ▪ Make sure dog crates are big enough for the animal to be comfortable. ▪ Allow only one dog per crate (although litters of puppies can usually be transported with several puppies per crate). ▪ Clean and disinfect crates between animals. ▪ If not in cage, the dog should be leashed or tethered inside the vehicle. ▪ Control climate within the vehicle. • Small dogs can become very cold. • Make sure dogs do not get overheated. ▪ Note: Keeping dogs inside stationary vehicles during hot weather can result in death.

Carrying Dogs

Transporting Dogs

INSTRUCTOR GUIDANCE	CONTENT
	Animal Handling: Cats **What is the best way to approach a cat?**

Suggested responses:

- Speak slowly, softly, and often.
- Approach with your side facing the cat.
- Move slowly.
- Work with a partner.

Display Slide 32

Present the information here if not already covered by the class.

- Speak slowly, softly, and often.
- Make yourself smaller by approaching with your side facing the cat.
- Move slowly.
- Work with a partner whenever possible.

Display Slide 33

Handling Out-of-Control Cats

- Back off and allow the cat to calm down.
- Use double thick or armored gloves and eye protection.
- Attempt capture with fishing nets, blankets, or traps.
- If possible, leave this job to professional animal handlers.

CERT Knowledge and Skills Involving Animals

INSTRUCTOR GUIDANCE	CONTENT

Display Slide 34

Transporting Cats

- Handling cats is easiest if the owner is present.
- Wear gloves, even with friendly cats.
- Towels can also be used to lift and carry cats.
- See if the cat will come to you. Try tapping a cat food can with a spoon.
- Pick up cats using as little restraint as needed, based on the cat's behavior and threat level.
- Be aware that cats may become frightened by unexpected stimuli such as loud noises or bright lights.
- Keep in mind that cats become defensive easily and can bite or scratch. Cat bites almost always become infected.
- Place cats in carriers for transporting. Placing a carrier with the opening upward and lowering the cat back feet first into the carrier often works best. Many cats resist being placed head first into carriers.
- If a carrier is not available, a pillowcase can be used to transport a cat in an emergency.

Display Slide 35

Animal Handling: Horses

- Control the head.
- Use a halter or lead rope.
- Be patient and careful.
- Keep your voice soft and soothing.
- Do not move suddenly.
- Be careful not to lose your temper as this usually makes the situation worse.

CERT Knowledge and Skills Involving Animals

INSTRUCTOR GUIDANCE	CONTENT

Display Slide 36

Animal Handling: Livestock

- Use a halter or lariat and wear gloves.

- Use proper footwear. Do not wear steel-toed boots.

- Wear heavy pants to protect yourself from scratches. Heavy pants can also offer some protection against kicks.

- Use radios and whistles for communication with other handlers.

- Make use of any fences, chutes, or panels that are available to help herd livestock.

- Use vehicles or people to form a line and herd livestock through a broken fence.

- Most herd animals move away from humans when approached. If you chase them, they will run.

Display Slide 37

Be creative in describing the types of temporary barricade material that could be used.

Herding and Containing Cattle

- Herd the animals toward containment using flags, hand-waving, or working dogs.

- Never lead cattle or cows unless they are show animals and are used to being led.

- Contain animals with portable barricades such as portable fencing or snow fence. Even survey or caution tape may help create temporary barriers until more appropriate containment can be created.

INSTRUCTOR GUIDANCE	CONTENT
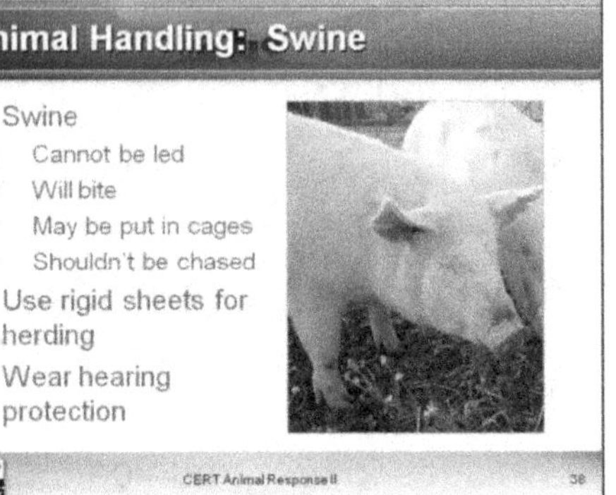 **Display Slide 38**	**Animal Handling: Swine** ▪ Pigs cannot be led. ▪ Pigs will bite. ▪ Smaller pigs may be put in cages or kennels. ▪ Avoid chasing pigs as they are subject to heat stress and could collapse or die if overexerted in a hot environment. ▪ You can use rigid sheets (plywood, corrugated sheeting) to herd pigs. ▪ Use hearing protection when working in close proximity to swine.
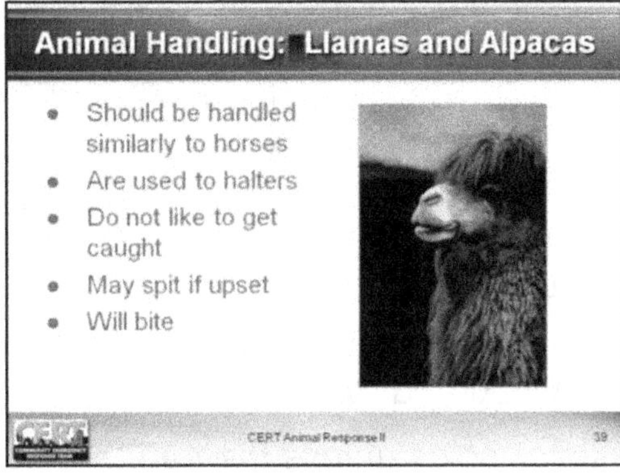 **Display Slide 39**	**Animal Handling: Llamas and Alpacas** ▪ Should be approached and handled more like horses than cattle ▪ Are usually used to halters ▪ Do not like to get caught ▪ May spit when upset ▪ Llamas have six canine teeth and will bite.
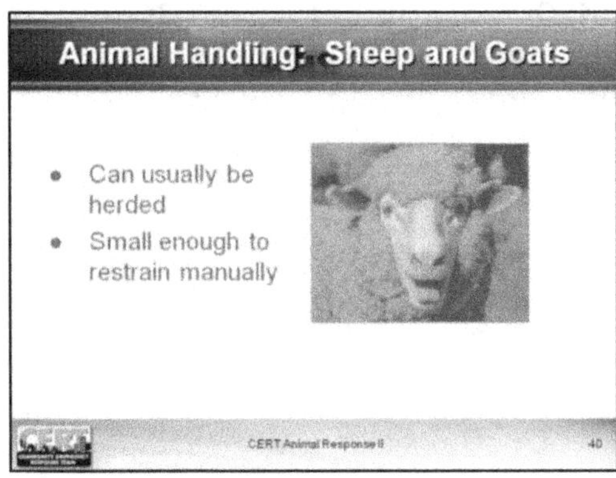 **Display Slide 40**	**Animal Handling: Sheep and goats** ▪ Can usually be herded ▪ Are small enough to restrain manually

CERT Knowledge and Skills Involving Animals

INSTRUCTOR GUIDANCE	CONTENT
	Ask participants if anyone has any questions about handling any of the animals covered thus far.

Display Slide 41

Insert specific animal handling techniques for any animal that is prevalent in the local wildlife or local agriculture, or any animal that is a common local pet.

Handling Exotic Animals and Other Species

Explain that birds, reptiles, amphibians, ferrets, rabbits, and rodents are temperature-sensitive and cannot get too cold or too hot. Many of these animals are also stress-sensitive and may be difficult to handle or dangerous.

Exotic animals

- Exotic animals are becoming increasingly common in the U.S. as pets.

- Exotic animal handling requires skilled professionals. Exotic animals can range from small and delicate to extremely dangerous. As with other animals, they could carry zoonotic diseases.

- Big cats are extremely dangerous and have no fear of people. They must be handled by experienced wildlife professionals, often with chemical capture.

- Wolves and wolf hybrids do NOT behave like dogs. They usually display timid pack behavior and may become aggressive if threatened or when protecting their pups.

- Venomous snakes or big cats may be used to guard drug operations.

- Birds can be aggressive and can use their beaks to bite or attack. Large birds, such as emus and ostriches, may kick; raptors may use their wings or talons as weapons.

- Monkeys and apes can be exceedingly strong and dangerous. Some can carry a deadly Herpes B virus that is a minor issue for them but fatal for people.

CERT Knowledge and Skills Involving Animals

INSTRUCTOR GUIDANCE	CONTENT

Display Slide 42

Explain that the next section will cover basic care for injured animals. Refer participants to p. 27 of the Participant Manual.

Caring for Injured Animals

Present the following information:

1. If no one is there to instruct you, act within the framework of your CERT training.

2. Perform sizeup to assess the situation.

3. Be careful — any stressed or injured animal may bite, scratch, kick, or otherwise injure you.

4. Restrain the animal appropriately before administering care.

5. If you are unable to restrain the animal, do not attempt to administer first aid.

6. If it is safe to do so, transport the animal for professional help.

Exercise: Caring for Injured Animals

Purpose: The purpose of this exercise is to let the class share their knowledge of caring for animals with each other.

Instructions: Follow the steps below to conduct the exercise:

1. Have the class break into teams of six people each.

Give each group an index card or a laminated card with a scenario.

The four scenarios appear on the following pages:

2. Assign a scenario to each team. Depending on the number of teams, more than one team may use the same scenario:

  a. A dog with heatstroke

  b. An iguana with hypothermia

  c. A foal with a bleeding leg

INSTRUCTOR GUIDANCE	CONTENT

a. You and your team members encounter a dog that is lying on the ground panting and breathing rapidly. The dog appears listless and lethargic. Your team determines that the animal has heat stroke. What can you do to care for the animal?
 	
 b. Your team has evacuated a family from their home to a hospital after a snowstorm that knocked down a portion of their house. As you are preparing to leave, you notice an aquarium with an iguana huddled at the side of the glass. On closer inspection, you realize the iguana is showing signs of hypothermia. What can you do to care for the animal?
 	
 c. Your team is inspecting the health of animals after a hurricane damaged a large horse stable. Local veterinarians have set up an animal triage station. The veterinarians are overworked with too many horses, and your team is asked to care for a small foal without much instruction. The foal has a large cut across its front leg. How can you care for this animal?
 	
 d. Your team has rescued a goat from a wildfire that spread through a local farm. You have transported the goat to safety. The animal is lying on
	d. A goat with burn wounds
	
	 3. Ask each group to come up with simple measures to care for the animal in its scenario. Have them record their response on a sheet of blank paper.
	
	 4. Ask each group to share its plan with the rest of the class.
	
	 5. After each group shares its response, add any of the following information that was not covered:
	
	 a. A dog with heatstroke
	   ■ Remove animal from hot environment.
	   ■ Apply alcohol to the pads of the feet (only for dogs and cats).
	   ■ Wet fur on extremities with cool water (do not use cold water).
	   ■ Transport for veterinary care as soon as possible.
	
	 b. An iguana with hypothermia
	   ■ Note: Hypothermia is more likely to affect reptiles, birds, and smaller animals.
	   ■ Evacuate the animal (with its cage if possible).
	   ■ Remove from cold environment.
	   ■ Provide indirect warmth (do not place animal directly on a heat source).
	
	 c. A foal with a bleeding leg
	   ■ Safely restrain the animal.
	   ■ Apply direct pressure.
	   ■ Bandage when practical.
	   ■ Do not remove any impaled objects.
	
	 d. A goat with burns
	   ■ Safely restrain the goat.
	   ■ Wet down potential burned areas with clean cool water, paying attention to the

INSTRUCTOR GUIDANCE	CONTENT
its side, conscious, but suffering numerous burns on its limbs, back, and stomach. What can you do to care for the animal?	torso. (In livestock, ashes and embers can settle in the fur on their backs.) • Note: Burns and wounds may not be readily noticeable in animals because they may be covered by fur. 6. Transport for veterinary care as soon as possible. Debrief: Remind the class that these exercises illustrate general techniques that CERT members can use to care for injured animals encountered during disaster. Refer participants to the list of organizations at the end of the Participant Manual for more detailed training on animal first aid.

Communicating with Animal Owners

Tell participants that the psychological strain on animal owners in a disaster may cause grief, anger, or irrational behavior. Refer them to Unit 7 on Disaster Psychology in their *CERT Basic Training* Participant Manuals to review that information.

Cover the following information:

The Human-Animal Bond

- Keeping humans with their pets can calm both.

- Livestock owners depend on their animals for their livelihood and also may be emotionally attached to their animals.

- Some animal owners and caretakers will not evacuate if they cannot take their animals with them.

- People may feel guilt over leaving animals behind.

Emotional Support for Animal Owners

Display Slide 43

CERT Knowledge and Skills Involving Animals

INSTRUCTOR GUIDANCE	CONTENT
	<ul><li>Consider the impact of separating people from their animals.</li><li>Understand that animal owners may be overly concerned with the care of their animals and neglect their own care or the care of their families.</li><li>Make sure the basic physical needs of humans are being met. (If physical needs are not met, people may become psychologically stressed.)</li><li>Be prepared to explain how the owner's animal will be cared for (correct information is a great stress reliever).</li><li>If a person is distressed over animal loss, listen and be compassionate.</li><li>In attempting to comfort the owner, do not promise anything you cannot deliver.</li></ul>
Be prepared to describe any local emergency plans related to animals.	Be sure to explain any plans or provisions already in place in the local community to help care for animals during an emergency, e.g., emergency animal shelter(s) that will be opened if an incident requires mass sheltering of people. Exercise: Communicating with Animal Owners Roleplay 1 Purpose: The purpose of this exercise is to allow participants to come up with communication strategies and critique communication skills.
Insert two disasters that are likely to occur locally.	Instructions: Follow the steps below to conduct the exercise. 1. Ask the class for a volunteer who is willing to practice his or her communication skills. Have the volunteer come to the front of the class. 2. Read the following scenario: You are attempting to evacuate a farmer from his home, but he refuses to leave. Most of the

INSTRUCTOR GUIDANCE	CONTENT
	community has already left as the evacuation was ordered almost 24 hours ago. A (insert local disaster) is approaching quickly, and the farmer's life will be at risk if he does not leave soon. You are unable to provide shelter for the farmer's 65 sheep, but you want the farmer to evacuate with you to an emergency shelter.

3. Ask the volunteer to play him- or herself while you play the role of the farmer. Let the participant know that he or she should try to convince you to leave for the emergency shelter now without taking care of your livestock.

4. Begin the roleplay by stating in an angry voice: "I refuse to leave my herd! I don't know what would happen to the sheep, and I cannot afford to lose even one of them."

5. Let the volunteer respond, and then say: "You disaster workers aren't good for anything! What good are you if you can't save my animals?"

6. Continue the conversation with two more statements such as, "What will I do if I lose all of my animals?" and "I would rather die than try to live without my farm."

7. End the roleplay by giving in and agreeing to go with the CERT volunteer.

8. Ask the class to critique the communication skills of the participant volunteer. What did the volunteer do right? What could have been done differently? Use the content in "Communicating with Animal Owners" above to aid the critique.

Debrief: Debrief by emphasizing the importance of using communication strategies to calm animal owners and de-escalate charged interactions.

INSTRUCTOR GUIDANCE	CONTENT
	<u>Exercise: Communicating with Animal Owners Roleplay 2</u> <u>Purpose:</u> The purpose of this exercise is to allow participants to come up with communication strategies and critique communication skills. <u>Instructions:</u> Follow the steps below to conduct the exercise. 1. Ask the class for a second volunteer who is willing to practice his or her communication skills. Have the volunteer come to the front of the class. 2. Read the following scenario: You are assisting in an emergency shelter until a (insert local disaster) passes. A family that owns two dogs has come to you asking how you think their dogs will be once the (insert disaster) has passed. The family was ordered to leave their dogs behind as animals are not allowed in the shelter. The family left the dogs inside their house with enough food and water to last for a week. The family consists of a mother, father, an 8-year-old boy, and a 5-year-old girl. The little boy is crying and moaning that the dogs are probably dead. 3. Ask the volunteer to play him- or herself while you play the role of the mother or father. Let the participant know that he or she should answer your questions as calmly and honestly as possible. 4. Begin the roleplay by asking in a distressed voice: "What do you think will happen to our dogs in the house by themselves for so long?" 5. Let the volunteer respond, and then say: "How long do you think we will be in here anyway? When is this all going to be over?" 6. Continue the conversation with two more statements such as, "What will my children do if

CERT Knowledge and Skills Involving Animals

CERT Knowledge and Skills Involving Animals

INSTRUCTOR GUIDANCE	CONTENT
	something happens to those dogs? They've grown up with them" or "How could you not have a shelter for pets? It's unthinkable!"
	7. End the roleplay by saying, "Okay, thanks for your help. Will you let us know as soon as you receive any new information?"
	8. Ask the class to critique the communication skills of the participant volunteer. What did the volunteer do right? What could have been done differently? Use the content in "Communicating with Animal Owners" above to aid the critique.
	<u>Debrief:</u> Debrief by emphasizing the importance of using communication strategies to calm animal owners and de-escalate charged interactions.
	Ask if anyone has any questions or comments about communicating with owners who are stressed about the well-being of their animals.

Animal Identification

Display Slide 44

Add information regarding a system or protocol for identifying dangerous animals in your community, if there is one.

Explain that, in the course of performing CERT functions, team members may not actually handle or provide care to every animal they encounter. However, in most encounters, team members will need to identify the animals and document them as accurately as possible.

Cover the following information:

Animals can be identified with tags, microchips, tattoos (generally on the lip, thigh, or ear), ear tags, bands (for birds), branding (on livestock), and collars.

Note that CERT members will rely on visible means of identification to document animals. These include: tags, ear tags, bands, branding, or collars.

There may be specialized systems for identifying dangerous animals in some communities. (Insert the system in your community if there is one.)

INSTRUCTOR GUIDANCE	CONTENT
Note: You may choose to substitute local forms to be used by CERT members for animal documentation. If so, be sure to replace the forms in the Participant Manual with local forms.	**Animal Documentation** Ask participants to review the sample documentation forms in the back of their Participant Manuals. Explain the following: • The data called for on each form • To whom the completed forms should be given, based on your local CERT program procedures Stress that ideally each form would have a photo attached of the animal or the animal with its owner. Whether or not a photo is possible, the form must be completed. **Ask participants if anyone has any questions about the documentation forms.** **Under what circumstances would you have to document animals?**
Suggested responses: • When an animal is displaced or lost • When an animal must be sheltered and the owner is unavailable or unable to give information	

CERT Knowledge and Skills Involving Animals

INSTRUCTOR GUIDANCE	CONTENT

	Sources for Additional Training and Information
	
	Let the class know that they can use the resources listed in their Participant Manuals to learn more about issues related to animal response and animal handling.
	
	Review these resources:
	
	American Humane Association
	
	- http://www.americanhumane.org/
	- Provides the following training:
	  - *Animal Shelter Disaster Preparedness*
	  - *Playful Parrots: Bird Care*
	  - *Safe Handling of Cats and Dogs*
	  - *Animal Rescue Training for First Responders*
	  - *Basic Animal Emergency Services Training*
	  - *Floodwater Rescue Operations for Animals*
	
	American Red Cross
	
	- http://www.redcross.org/
	- Provides *Pet First Aid* publication
	
	American Veterinary Medical Association
	
	- http://www.avma.org/
	- Provides the following publications:
	  - *AVMA Disaster Preparedness and Response Guide*
	  - *Saving the Whole Family*
	  - *Disaster Preparedness for Veterinary Practices*
	
	Animal Control Agencies (State and Local)
	
	- May provide animal handling training
	- Course topics vary by location

Sources for Additional Training and Information

INSTRUCTOR GUIDANCE	CONTENT
	Basic Animal Rescue Training (BART) http://basicanimalrescuetraining.org/ <ul><li>Provides the following training:<ul><li>*BART Small Animal*</li><li>*BART Community Responder*</li><li>*BART Large Animal*</li></ul></li></ul>**Code 3 Associates**<ul><li>http://www.code3associates.org/</li><li>Provides the following training:<ul><li>*Technical Animal Rescue (TAR)*</li><li>*BULL/Large Animal Rescue*</li><li>*ICE Rescue*</li><li>*Bio-Security and Zoonoses*</li></ul></li></ul>**Department of Homeland Security Center for Domestic Preparedness**<ul><li>http://cdp.dhs.gov/</li><li>Provides *Agricultural Emergency Response Training (AgERT-B)*</li></ul>**Department of Homeland Security/Federal Emergency Management Agency**<ul><li>http://www.training.fema.gov/IS/</li><li>Provides the following on-line training:<ul><li>IS-10 Animals in Disasters Module A: Awareness and Preparedness</li><li>IS-11 Animals in Disasters Module B: Community Planning</li><li>IS-111 Livestock in Disasters</li></ul></li></ul>**Extension Disaster Education Network (EDEN)**<ul><li>http://eden.lsu.edu/</li><li>Provides *Animal Agrosecurity and Emergency Management* training</li></ul>

INSTRUCTOR GUIDANCE	CONTENT

	The Humane Society of the United States
	
	- http://www.hsus.org/
	- Provides the following training:
	  - *Disaster Animal Response Team (DART)* training
	  - *Emergency Animal Sheltering (EAS)* training
	
	University Extension Service
	
	- May provide livestock handling training
	- Course topics vary by location

Display Slide 45	## Module Summary Summarize the topics that were discussed in this module. ### The Role of CERT in Responding to Animal Issues CERT members support various disaster response personnel and may be called upon to assist in a variety of animal-related tasks. CERT members may be faced with animal encounters during emergency functions that do not appear to be animal-related tasks. Understanding the CERT role in functions involving animals will help prepare team members for the varying situations they may encounter. ### CERT Responder Safety When Dealing With Animals CERT members may encounter animals in numerous situations. It is important to know safety precautions in advance.

INSTRUCTOR GUIDANCE	CONTENT
	Knowledge and Skills Needed for CERT Functions That May Involve Animals Emergency situations involving animals require preparation and practice. Skills include maintaining personal safety, basic animal care and handling, communicating with animal owners, and documenting animals you encounter. *CERT Animal Response I* and *II* have provided information and training about animal behavior and animal handling techniques to help prepare participants for the situations they may encounter during a disaster. **Sources for Additional Training and Information** Encourage participants to consider related training available from the organizations listed in the Participant Manual.
	Closing **Ask if anyone has any final questions.** Thank participants for attending the training. Remind participants of any upcoming training or other local CERT program events.

Module Summary

Displaced Animal Documentation Checklist

If the animal cannot be contained, document and report to local animal professionals:

Last known location: ____

Physical description: ____

Disposition: ____

If the animal can be contained, assure that the animal is tagged. If needed, tag the animal using whatever means possible (such as duct tape). Take a photo if possible and attach photo to the form. Document the following:

Location found: ____

Time and date found: ____

Physical description and breed: ____

Identifying marks or tags: ____

Current location: ____

Reported bite history: ____

Condition upon intake: ____

Observed behavior traits: ____

Owned Animal Documentation Checklist

If an animal is owned and being sheltered, contained, or cared for, take a photo of the owner with the animal if possible and attach to the form. Document the following:

Owner's name: ____

Home address: ____

Current contact information: ____________________________________

Physical description of animal: __________________________________

Vaccination history: ____

Observable physical condition: __________________________________

Current medical conditions and medications needed: _________________

Identification: ____

Behavioral traits: ____

Feeding schedule: ____

Food and special dietary needs: _________________________________

Bite history: ____

Notes

Notes

www.ingramcontent.com/pod-product-compliance
Lightning Source LLC
Chambersburg PA
CBHW080034260726
48658CB00007B/2610